Mechanics,
The Ultimate Collection of Mechanic Jokes

Published by Glowworm Press
7 Nuffield Way
Abingdon OX14 1RL
By Chester Croker

Jokes For Mechanics

These jokes for mechanics will make you giggle. Some of them are old, which we have repaired, some of them are new and hopefully they will provide a bright spark in your day.
These funny mechanical gags have been put together to get you roaring like an engine with laughter.

Disclaimer
All rights reserved. No part of this publication may be reproduced in any form or by any means without the written permission of the publisher. The information herein is offered for informational purposes only, and is universal as so. The presentation of the information is without contract or any type of guarantee assurance. Under no circumstances will any legal responsibility or blame be held against the author for any reparation, damages or monetary loss due to the information herein, either directly or indirectly.

FOREWORD

When I was asked to write a foreword to this book I was thrilled.

That is until I was told that I was the last resort by the author, Chester Croker, and that everyone else he had approached had said they couldn't do it!

I will give him a *brake* though, as he *wipes me out* with his gags, and I often end up *exhausted* with laughter.

I have known Chester for a number of years and his ability to create funny jokes is absolutely incredible. He is quick witted and an expert at crafting clever puns and amusing gags and I feel he is the ideal man to put together a joke book about our profession.

He will be glad you have bought this book, as he has an expensive lifestyle to maintain.

Enjoy!

Jack Hammer

Table of Contents

Chapter 1: Introduction

Chapter 2: One Liner Mechanic Jokes

Chapter 3: Question and Answer Mechanic Jokes

Chapter 4: Short Mechanic Jokes

Chapter 5: Longer Mechanic Jokes

Chapter 6: Mechanics Pick-Up Lines

Chapter 7: Bumper Stickers for Mechanics

Chapter 1: Mechanics Jokes

Every mechanic needs a laugh every now and then to make work go quicker, right?

If you are looking for funny mechanic jokes, you're in the right place. From hilarious one-liners and comical, engaging long form jokes to some cheesy mechanic pick-up lines, we've got the jokes guaranteed to make you laugh out loud.

Mechanics know that their customers all have varying degrees of knowledge about their vehicles. While some people don't have a clue what goes on under the hood, others know just enough to get themselves into trouble – and that's how some of the best mechanic jokes are born.

OK, onto the jokes.

Chapter 2: One Liner Mechanic Jokes

It takes 8,460 bolts to assemble an automobile, but only one nut to scatter it all over the road.

The easiest way to make your old car run better is to check prices of a new car.

Is it just me who has spent more on my tool box than my car?

Did you hear about the miracle of the blind mechanic?

He picked up a hammer and saw.

My greatest fear is that when I die my wife will sell all my car parts for what I told her they cost.

I got called pretty yesterday and it felt good. Actually, the full sentence was "You're a pretty bad mechanic." but I'm choosing to focus on the positive.

The number one indication that you will need a mechanic is when someone says to you: "My brother-in-law used to be a mechanic and he reckons the problem is……."

My mechanic tried to convince me that my car needs new brakes, but I know that it would just slow me down.

I'm moving up in my career as a bike mechanic - I've been promoted to spokes-person.

Did you hear about the car mechanic who was in a brief relationship and then left? There was an article in the newspaper.

A jump starter cable goes into a bar and the bartender says," I'll serve you, but don't start anything."

I recently got a new Korean mechanic but it's hard to understand him - he speaks with a Hyundai Accent!

I've never once been able to explain my car trouble to a mechanic without resorting to sound effects.

A tree never hits an automobile - except in self defense.

A mechanic wanted to buy something nice for his boss, so he bought him a new chair. His boss won't let him plug it in though.

A mechanic fell onto his tools - it was a gut-wrenching experience.

If Apple made cars, would they have Windows?

One day, a mechanic's wife asked him to pass her lipstick but he passed her a glue stick instead by mistake. She still isn't talking to him.

Did you hear about the cross-eyed mechanic who got sacked because he couldn't see eye to eye with his customers?

A mechanic friend of mine gave me some great advice, saying I should put something away for a rainy day. I've gone for an umbrella.

I went to pick up my car and the mechanic told me, "I couldn't fix the brakes so I made the horn louder."

Chapter 3: Question and Answer Jokes

Q: What does a lesbian have in common with a mechanic?
A: They both have Snap-on tools!

Q: What do you call an Oscar winning film about mechanics?
A: Lord of the Springs.

Q: Did you hear about the mechanic with a fear of commitment?
A: He likes to screw, nut and bolt.

Q: What do you call a man with a car on his head?

A: Jack.

Q: How can you tell if a mechanic has just had sex?
A: One of his fingers is clean.

Q: How do you tell a gamer from a car mechanic?
A: Ask them both what HP means.

Q: Why did the cannibal mechanic get disciplined by his boss?
A: For buttering up the customers.

Q: What did the arts graduate say to the mechanic?
A: Would you like fries with that?

Q: Why did Walt Disney visit a mechanic?

A: Because he wanted to get his car-tooned.

Q: Why did the tractor trailer mechanic always have half an erection?
A: Because he was constantly nursing a semi.

Q: What's the difference between a mechanic and a priest?
A: The mechanic waits until you've grown up to have sex with you.

Q: Why do babies make bad mechanics?
A: They have poorly developed motor skills.

Q: What do you call a guy with his hand up a camel's arse?
A: An Arab mechanic.

Q: What kind of mechanics fix and break your car at the same time?

A: Quantum Mechanics.

Q: What's the difference between a mechanic and a doctor?
A: Mechanics wash their hands before they pee.

Q: How many auto mechanics does it take to change a light bulb?
A: Two. One to force it with a hammer and the other to go out for more bulbs.

Q: What do you call a movie about bad mechanics?
A: The Last and the Furious.

Q: What do you call a cross-dressing car dent repair technician?

A: A gender-bender fender-mender.

Q: What's the difference between a bad mechanic and a politician?
A: With a mechanic, there's a good chance something might get fixed.

Q: What does a mechanic do in a one night stand?
A: He nuts and bolts.

Q: What do you call a Greek mechanic?
A: A Greece monkey.

Q: What do you call a mechanic who is happy every Monday?

A: Retired.

Chapter 4: Short Mechanic Jokes

A dumb blonde pushes her BMW into the gas station and tells the mechanic that it died.

After working on it for a few minutes, he has it idling smoothly.

"What's the story?" she asked.

"Just crap in the carburettor," the mechanic replied.

"How often do I have to do that?" asked the blonde.

A guy walks into an auto shop and says, "I'd like a new exhaust for my KIA."

The car mechanic thinks for a few seconds then says, "Ok, that seems like a fair trade."

A dog walks into a pub, and takes a seat. He says to the barman, "Can I have a pint of lager and a packet of crisps please."

The barman says, "Crikey, that's amazing - you should join the circus.'"

The talking dog replies, "Why? Do they need car mechanics?"

A mechanic in my area went to jail for dealing drugs.

I've been one of his customers for over five years and I had no clue he was a mechanic.

The definition of a mechanic's knife: A tool that is used to open and slice through the contents of cardboard cartons delivered to your front door; works particularly well on boxes containing convertible tops or tonneau covers.

A guy took his 1973 Volkswagen Beetle to an auto repair shop and said "My engine is missing."

The blonde mechanic raised the hood and said "Oh wow, you're right! But how the heck did you drive it here?"

An Eskimo goes to the mechanic and the mechanic says "It looks like you blew a seal" to which the eskimo replies "No, that's just frost on my mustache."

Two mechanics are talking about sex.

The first mechanic says that sex is 75% work and 25% pleasure. The second mechanic says that sex is 25% work and 75% pleasure.

At a standstill, they decide to ask their apprentice's opinion.

"Sex is all pleasure" says the apprentice.

"Why do you say that?" ask the mechanics.

The apprentice replies "Well, if there is any work involved, you two have me do it."

A roofer was replacing some tiles on a mechanic's house.

The roofer accidentally cuts off his ear, and yells down "Look out for my ear I just cut off."

The mechanic looks around and calls up "Is this your ear?"

The roofer looks down and replies "Nope. Mine had a pencil behind it!"

A mechanic showed up late for work one day. His boss was concerned so he asked, "Why were you late today?" to which the mechanic replied, "I could have been here sooner but my timing was retarded."

This mechanic says to a puzzled young guy "Can I help you?"

To which the young guy replies "My car won't start."

The mechanic says to the guy "Umm, that's a bicycle."

The young guy answers back "Yes, that's because my car won't start."

A hard working mechanic complained to his friend that his wife doesn't satisfy him anymore.

His buddy told him he needed to find another woman on the side, pretty sharpish.

When they met up a month or so later, the mechanic told his buddy "I took your advice. I actually managed to find two women on the side, but my wife still doesn't satisfy me!"

A mechanic goes to the doctor with a hearing problem.

The doctor says, "Can you describe the symptoms to me?"

The mechanic replies "Yes. Homer is a fat yellow lazy man and his wife Marge is skinny with big blue hair."

A mechanic calls up his local paper and asks "How much would it be to put an ad in your paper?"

"Four dollars an inch," a woman replies. "Why? What are you selling?"

"An eight-foot extendable ladder," said the mechanic before slamming the phone down.

A blonde meets up with a friend as she's picking up her car from the mechanic.

"Everything ok with your car now?" the friend asks.

"Yes, thank goodness," the blonde replies.

"Weren't you worried the mechanic might try to rip you off?" asks her friend.

The blonde replies "Yes, but he didn't. I was so relieved when he told me that all I needed was blinker fluid!"

A Paladin takes his car to a mechanic and says, "Whenever I'm driving, I get these strange urges to run over pedestrians."

The mechanic has a look under the car and replies, "Your alignment is off."

A mechanic is struggling to find a parking space.

"Lord," he prayed. "I can't stand this much longer. If you open a space up for me, I swear I'll give up the booze and go to church every single Sunday."

Suddenly, the clouds part and the sun shines down on an empty parking spot.

Without hesitation, the mechanic says: "Never mind Lord, I found one."

An elderly dyslexic gentleman drops his precious Cadillac off and instructs the chief mechanic, "Don't forget to change out the headlight oil and turn signal coolant, they help the Cadillac converter run good."

A mechanic is sitting at the bar after work one night, when a big, sweaty construction worker sits down next to him.

They start talking, have a few beers and the conversation gets on to nuclear war.

The mechanic asks the construction worker, "If you hear the sirens go off, the missiles are on their way, and you've only got 20 minutes left to live, what would you do?"

The construction worker replies, "That's easy - I'm going make it with anything that moves."

The construction worker then asks the mechanic what he would do to which he replies, "I'm going to try and keep perfectly still."

I never knew my mechanic was a psychic until he loudly announced that I had blown a tranny in my car.

A doctor says to a car mechanic, "Your fee is several times more per hour then we get paid for medical care."

The mechanic replies, "Yeah, but you see, doc, you always work on the same model, it hasn't changed since Adam's time; but we have to keep up to date with new models coming out every year."

As a mechanic I can safely say I don't understand the gay agenda.

However, I do understand the Trans mission.

A mechanic tries to enter a smart bar wearing a shirt open at the collar, and is met by a bouncer who tells him that he must wear a necktie to gain admission.

So the mechanic goes to his car to try and find a necktie but he can't find one.

However he knows he has some jump leads; and so he ties these around his neck, and manages to fashion a fairly acceptable looking knot with the ends dangling free.

He goes back to the bar and the bouncer carefully looks him over, and then says: "Well, OK, I guess you can come in now - just don't start anything!"

A blonde walks into a mechanic's shop she is worried nobody will want to buy her car as it has done a lot of miles.

The mechanic tells her that for a price, he can roll back the odometer. After she agrees, he does just that, and he tells her she can now sell her car.

The blonde says, "Why would I do that? My car has much lower mileage now!"

A gynecologist decided to become a mechanic.

He graduated mechanic school and he asked his teacher how he managed to get such good grades.

The teacher said "Well, you did well in the written exam and then you reassembled the motor perfectly, and we had to give you the extra credit when you did it all through the Muffler!"

A mechanic took his cross-eyed dog to the vet.

The vet picked the dog up to examine him and said, "Sorry, I'm going to have to put him down."

The mechanic said, "It's not that bad is it?"

The vet replied, "No, he's just very heavy."

A priest goes to a mechanic to get his tires rotated on his car, and as the car is about to be lowered from the lift, the priest asks the mechanic, "Are those lugnuts tight enough?"

The mechanic replies, "Tighter than a nun's c**t, Father."

"You best give them another tug then, son." says the priest.

A retired mechanic was walking along the road one day when he came across a frog.

He reached down, picked the frog up, and started to put it in his pocket.

As he did so, the frog said, "Kiss me on the lips and I'll turn into a really hot woman and show you a very good time."

The ex-mechanic carried on putting the frog in his pocket.

The frog said, "Didn't you hear what I said?"

The old mechanic looked at the frog and said, "Yes, but at my age I'd rather have a talking frog."

A mobile mechanic was working on my car in my driveway.

I had just finished washing the floor when he asked to use the toilet.

With dismay I looked at his muddy boots and my newly polished floor.

"Just a minute," I said, "I'll put down some newspaper."

"That's all right, madam" he responded. "I'm house trained."

Chapter 5: Longer Mechanic Jokes

Hot Lips

A girl is driving along the road listening to the radio when she hears a song she really likes. When the song is over the announcer says the title of the record was, "Hot Lips and Tender Kisses."
When she gets home she's excited about the new song and decides to call her local music store to see if they have the record.
Hurriedly, and excitedly, she dials the store's number. But in her excitement, she unknowingly misdialled and got an auto repair shop instead.
"Hello," the mechanic answers.
"Do you have Hot Lips and Tender Kisses?" the girl asks.
The mechanic was puzzled, but says, "Well, no, but I've got hot pants and seven inches."
"Oh, is that a record?" she says.
"No," he says, "but it's better than average."

The Heart Surgeon

A mechanic was removing a cylinder head from the engine of a Range Rover when he spotted a well-known heart surgeon in his shop. The surgeon was there waiting for the service manager to take a look at his Mercedes when the mechanic shouted across the garage: "Hey doc, can I ask you a question?"

The surgeon, a bit surprised, walked over to where the mechanic was working on the Range Rover.

The mechanic straightened up, wiped his hands on a rag and asked, "So Doc, look at this engine. I open its heart, take the valves out, repair any damage, and then put them back in, and when I finish, it works just like new. So why do I get an average salary and you get the really big money, when you and I are doing basically the same work?"

The surgeon paused, smiled and leaned over and whispered to the mechanic: "Try doing it with the engine running."

The To Do List

Here is a list of problems reported in our car shop for the mechanics to fix followed by the notes the mechanics left for the next shift to read the next morning.

Customer: Left inside main tire almost needs replacement.
Mechanic: Almost replaced left inside main tire.

Customer: Something loose in cabin.
Mechanic: Something tightened in cabin.

Customer: Evidence of leak on right hand side of engine.
Mechanic: Evidence removed.

Customer: Radio volume unbelievably loud.
Mechanic: Radio volume set to more believable level.

The Penguin

It's a really hot day and this penguin is having car trouble, so he takes it into a garage.
The penguin asks, "How long will it be?"
The mechanic says, "An hour or so."
So the penguin decides to go get an ice cream at the grocery store across the street.
When the penguin gets there he climbs inside the big freezer door and starts to eat ice cream.
Three hours go by before the penguin looks at his watch and jumps out of the freezer and races back to the garage.
With ice cream all over his face and his stomach he says, "So, how's my car?"
The mechanic comes walking out wiping his hands on a rag and says, "Looks like you blew a seal."
The penguin says, "No, no, no, I was just eating ice cream."

Water in the Carb

A teenage boy tells his father, "Dad, there's trouble with the car, it has water in the carburetor."

The father looks confused and says, "Water in the carburetor, that's ridiculous."

The son insists. "I tell you, the car has water in the carburetor."

His father, starting to get a little nervous, says "You don't even know what a carburetor is, but I will check it out. Where is the car?"

The son replies, "In the pool."

The Lincoln

I get in my friend's new car, a brand-new Lincoln, and right away I notice that it's a stick-shift.
I said, "You bought a new Lincoln with a stick shift? I didn't know that they made a Lincoln like that."
"They don't," he said. "I ordered it special."
"I'll bet that cost a fortune," I replied.
"Oh, yeah. You got that right," he told me.
"Why would you buy a new Lincoln with a stick shift?" I asked.
He said, "My wife can't drive a stick."

The Rust Bucket

A college student drove his ratty, raggedy old car into the mechanic's shop, needing some repair advice for his really old rust bucket. The mechanic looked at it for a couple of minutes and said, "What you really need is the radiator cap solution."

"Oh," said the student, trying not to sound too confused, "Do you mean the radiator cap isn't holding enough pressure?"

"That's part of the problem," the mechanic said. "You need to lift the radiator cap and drive another car under it. Then you can replace the radiator cap, and it should solve your problem."

The 710 Cap

The other day I was in the local auto parts store. A lady came in and asked for a seven ten cap. We all looked at each other and one of the service guys asked, "What's a seven ten cap?" She replied, "You know, it's right on the engine. Mine got lost somehow and I need a new one."
"What kind of car do you drive?" another guy asked. (Thinking that perhaps she drove an old Datsun Seven Ten.) The lady replied, "I drive a Buick." We asked her, how big is the cap? She made a circle with her hands about 3 1/2 inches in diameter.
"What does it do?" asked one of the service guys. She replied, "I don't know, but it's always been there."
One of the guys gave her a note pad and asked her if she could draw a picture of it. So she made a circle about 3 1/2 inches in diameter and in the center she wrote 710.
As she was drawing, the guys behind the counter looked at it upside down and they starting laughing out loud.
(Directions: Draw a circle and write 710 in the center. Now look at it upside down.)

Reunion

A group of mechanics, all aged 40, discussed where they should meet for a reunion lunch. They agreed they would meet at a place called The Dog House because the barmaids had big breasts and wore short-skirts.

Ten years later, at age 50, the friends discussed where they should meet for lunch.
They agreed that they would meet at The Dog House because the food and service was good and there was an excellent beer selection.

Ten years later, at age 60, the mechanics discussed where they should meet for lunch.
They agreed that they would meet at The Dog House because there were plenty of parking spaces, they could dine in peace and quiet, and it was good value for money.

Ten years later, at age 70, the friends discussed where they should meet for lunch.
They agreed that they would meet at The Dog House because the restaurant was wheelchair accessible and had a toilet for the disabled.

Ten years later, at age 80, the mechanics, now all retired, discussed where they should meet for lunch.

They agreed that they would meet at The Dog House because they had never been there before.

An Engineer, a Physicist and a Mechanic

An engineer, a physicist and a mechanic were having an argument as to who was the smartest. One of them proposed a contest to settle the matter once and for all.

For the contest, each of them would be locked in a room with three ball bearings for one week. At the end of the week they would see what each of them could do with their ball bearings.

At the end of the week, they opened the door where the engineer was and found that he had all three ball bearings stacked one on top of the other, perfectly balanced.

They opened the door where the physicist was and discovered that he had all three ball bearings in orbits around one another.

Then they opened the door where the mechanic was and he had lost one, bent one and one was in his tool box.

The Sports Mechanic

Three middle-aged women are sitting on a park bench discussing their children.
"My son William studied Architecture at Cambridge. He's 25 years old now and he makes $70,000 a year at Bregmann and Hamann." the first woman says.
"My son Charlie read Law at Harvard. He'll be turning 23 in October and he makes $100,000 a year at Shoe Lane Chambers." says the second woman.
"My son Max didn't go to university. He left school at the age of 16, as a matter of fact. He's 30 now, but he makes half a million a year working as a sports mechanic in London." the third woman says.
"I've heard of car mechanics, plane mechanics and typewriter mechanics, but not a sports mechanic. What's that?" the first woman asks.
The third woman replies, "Well, he fixes rugby matches, football matches, tennis matches..."

A Mechanic Changes His Job

A mechanic had been unemployed for a rather long time and decided to open a medical clinic. Outside the clinic he put a sign that read: 'A cure for your ailment guaranteed at $500; we'll pay you $1,000 if we fail.'

A doctor sees this and thinks this is a good opportunity to make an easy $1,000. So he goes into the clinic.

Doctor: "I have lost my sense of taste."

Mechanic: "Nurse, please bring the medicine from box 22 and put 3 drops in the patient's mouth."

The nurse does as requested.

Doctor: "This is gasoline."

Mechanic: "Congratulations. You've got your sense of taste back. That will be $500."

The doctor gets annoyed and decides to go back several days later to recover his money.

Doctor: "I have lost my memory, I cannot remember anything."

Mechanic: "Nurse, please bring me the medicine from box 22 and put 3 drops in the patient's mouth."

Doctor: "But that's gasoline."

Mechanic: "Congratulations. You've got your memory back. That will be $500."

The doctor leaves angry that he is now $1,000 out of pocket. After several days he comes back, determined to get his money back.
Doctor: "My eyes, they're weak, I can't see a thing."
Mechanic: "Well, I don't have any medicine for that. Take this $1000 check."
The mechanic hands the doctor a check for $5.
Doctor: "But this is just $5."
Mechanic: "Congratulations – you've got your vision back. That will be $500."

Golfing Buddies

A pastor, a doctor and a mechanic were waiting one morning for a particularly slow group of golfers in front of them.
The mechanic fumed, "What's with these guys? We must have been waiting for ten minutes on each hole."
The doctor chimed in, "I don't know, but I've never seen any group so slow in my life."
The pastor said, "Here comes the greens keeper. Let's have a word with him."
The greens keeper explains, "Yes, they are slow. They are a group of blind firefighters and we let them play for free anytime."
The group was silent for a moment.
The pastor then said, "That's so sad. I think I will say a special prayer for them tonight."
The doctor said, "Good idea. And I'm going to contact my ophthalmologist buddy and see if there's anything he can do for them."
The mechanic said, "Why can't these guys play at night?"

A Mechanic Meets Satan

A mechanic dies, and, not being a very religious man, gets sent to Hell.
The mechanic meets Satan, who shows him the ins and outs of Hell.
While wandering around, the mechanic starts doing the thing he's best at - fixing stuff. In a matter of weeks, Hell has air conditioning, working TVs and indoor plumbing, all being maintained and improved by the mechanic.
Seeing this from heaven, God calls Satan over and demands to have the mechanic because Hell is supposed to be an awful place and shouldn't have any luxuries.
Satan refuses, and God threatens to sue him for the mechanic.
"Sue me?" Satan asks. "Where are you going to find a lawyer?"

Brake Fluid

One day a mechanic was working under a car when some brake fluid dripped into his mouth. 'Wow! That stuff isn't too bad tasting,' he thought.
The next day, he told his buddy about his tasting the brake fluid and told him "It was pretty good, actually. I think I'll have a little more today."
His friend was a little concerned, but didn't say anything.
The next day the mechanic told his buddy, "I drank a whole glass of brake fluid today. It tasted great."
A few days later, he was up to a bottle a day.
"You know," said his buddy, "that brake fluid is poison and really bad for you. You better cut out drinking that stuff."
The mechanic replied, "It's not a problem. I can stop any time!"

Three Friends

Ron is talking to two of his friends, Jim and Shamus.

Jim says, "I think my wife is having an affair with a mechanic. The other day I came home and found a socket set under our bed and it wasn't mine."

Shamus then confides, "Well I think my wife is having an affair with an electrician. The other day I found some wire cutters under the bed and they weren't mine."

Ron thinks for a minute and then says, "You know - I think my wife is having an affair with a horse."

Both Jim and Shamus stare at him in complete disbelief.

Ron sees them both looking at him and he says, "No, seriously. The other day I came home early and found a jockey under our bed."

Accident On An Oil Rig

There once was a young mechanic named Eric, who got a job on an off-shore oil rig.
He devoted himself to doing the best job he could to assist with the maintenance of all the machinery. He looked after the power generators, the pumps, the hydraulic systems and even did a little work on the electric systems.
One day, Eric was working on the power generator when tragedy struck. He had begun to hoist a cylinder head when next thing anyone knew, the hoist had collapsed, landing on top of poor Eric's arms and severing them.
The medical team came to do the best for Eric, but they had to admit defeat. There was nothing they could do to save Eric's hands. Yet despite all of this, everyone was amazed with Eric's unperturbed calm.
When they asked him why he did not appear to be upset, he responded that "It was unfortunate, but it's not something I'm going to be writing home about."

The Parrot and the Mechanic

A mobile mechanic is called to the house of a cute little old lady. There is a restless Doberman sitting in the kitchen drooling and growling under his breath, and a parrot whistling contentedly next to him on his perch.
Half-way through the job, the little old lady tells him she's going to the grocery store. The mechanic asks the little old lady if he will be safe while she's away to which she smiles and says: "Oh yes. Poopsie is so sweet. He wouldn't hurt a fly. He's a good doggie."
Then the old lady adds: "Oh. But whatever you do, do NOT say anything to the parrot!"
Relieved, the mechanic resumes his work on the car. After the little old lady leaves, the parrot starts making a horrible racket and is calling the mechanic all manner of rude names.
The mechanic cannot concentrate on his work. Losing his temper, the mechanic glares at the bird and screams: "Shut up, you feathered fool!" and goes back to his work.
The bird is stunned into silence.
A few seconds later, the parrot squawks: "Stick it to him, Poopsie!"

The Pearly Gates

A mechanic dies in a fishing accident on his 60th birthday and finds himself greeted at the Pearly Gates by a brass band.
Saint Peter runs over, shakes his hand and says "Congratulations!"
"Congratulations for what?" asks the mechanic.
"We are celebrating the fact that you lived to be 100 years old." says Saint Peter.
"But that's not true," says the mechanic. "I only lived to be sixty."
"That's impossible," says Saint Peter, "we added up your labor hours booked on your invoices!"

Three Daughters

A dopey mechanic was talking to two of his friends about their teenage daughters.

The first friend says "I was cleaning my daughter's room the other day and I found a pack of cigarettes. I didn't even know she smoked."

The second friend says, "That's nothing. I was cleaning my daughter's room the other day and I found a half full bottle of Vodka. I didn't even know she drank."

The mechanic says, "That's nothing. I was cleaning my daughter's room the other day and I found a pack of condoms. I didn't even know she had a penis."

Dent Repair Technician

A blonde goes to a mechanic to ask about fixing dents in her car.
She asks the mechanic "How can I fix the dents myself as I have no money to pay for the repairs?"
The mechanic tells her "Just blow into the exhaust pipe as hard as you can and the dents will disappear."
So the blonde goes home and starts blowing into the exhaust pipe.
Another blonde is walking by and asks what she is doing.
The first blonde says, "I am getting rid of the dents by blowing into the exhaust. All the air will go inside the car and pop out the dents."
"That's not how to fix dents." responds the other blonde. "You've got to close the windows first so all the air doesn't escape!"

The Old Man

A guy is driving down the road when he sees an old man sitting on a stump, crying his eyes out. So the guy stops his car and asks the old man what's the matter.

"I've had a great life," says the old man. "I was a successful mechanic, and I sold my company to a large auto repair company for loads of money."

The guy says, "So what's the problem?"

The old man snuffles into his sleeve and says, "I built myself a large house with a swimming pool."

The younger guy looks puzzled and says, "Okay, so what's the problem?"

The old man wails and says, "I own two fantastic cars."

The younger guy scratches his head and says, "I don't see what the problem is."

The old man blows his nose and says, "Last month I got married to a 22 year old Playboy bunny."

The guy loses his temper. "Crikey, old man – what is your problem?"

The old man sobs, "I just can't remember where I live!"

Pulling Power

Carlo the property developer and his mechanic buddy Pete, went bar-hopping every week together, and every week Carlo would go home with a woman while Pete would go home alone. One week Pete asked Carlo his secret to picking up women.

"That's easy," said Carlo "When she asks you what you do for a living, don't tell her you're a mechanic. Tell her you're a lawyer instead."

Later Pete is dancing with a woman when she leans in and asks him what he does for a living.

"I'm a lawyer," Pete tells her.

The woman smiles flirtatiously and asks, "Shall we go to my place? It's just around the corner."

They go back to her place, have some fun and an hour later, Pete is back in the pub telling Carlo about his success.

"I've only been a lawyer for an hour," Pete snickered, "And I've already screwed someone!"

Exact Words

A wealthy sports car owner was delighted with the way the mechanic had tuned his car.
"You did a great job." he said and paid the mechanic for his work. "Also, in order to thank you, here's an extra 100 dollars to take the missus out to dinner."
Later that night, the doorbell rang and it was the mechanic.
Thinking the mechanic had forgotten something the car owner simply asked, "What's the matter, did you forget something?"
"Nope." replied the mechanic, "I'm just here to take your missus out to dinner like you asked."

Train Passengers

A mechanic, a tyre fitter, a beautiful lady, and an old woman were on a train, sitting 2x2 facing each other.

The train went into a tunnel and when the carriage went completely dark, a loud "smack" was heard. When the train came out of the tunnel back into the light the tyre fitter had a red hand print on his face. He had been slapped on the face.

The old lady thought, "That tyre fitter must have groped the young lady in the dark and she slapped him."

The hottie thought, "That tyre fitter must have tried to grope me, got the old lady by mistake, and she slapped him."

The tyre fitter thought, "That mechanic must have groped the hottie, she thought it was me, and slapped me."

The mechanic just sat there thinking, "I can't wait for another tunnel so I can slap that tyre fitter again!"

Chapter 6: Mechanic Pick-Up Lines

Would you like to lubricate my camshaft?

Is your battery dead? Cause I'd love to jump you.

It looks like I've got a stripped screw - want to help me pry it loose?

Your father must have been a mechanic because you have a finely tuned body.

If you were a car door, I'd slam you all night long.

I'd love to jack you up and check out your undercarriage.

Can you help me reconfigure my GPS system? I need directions to get into your pants.

I need some coolant, because you've got my engine overheating.

I'm lost, can you tell me which road leads to your heart?

Do you mind if I check out your exhaust pipe?

Ever had sex in bucket seats?

Do you know what the difference is between you and my car? I'd love to wreck you.

My nuts are made of titanium.

Hey baby, if you were a car, I'd be willing to pay for new headlights.

Hey baby, if you were a car, I'd check your oil regularly.

Who needs oil when you're naturally charged?

Will I get a chance to pop your clutch?

Would you like to blow my head gasket?

Would you like to improve my fuel economy?

Would you like to lubricate my camshaft?

You have a hybrid? You're so unconventional. I like that.

You make me glow as bright as your dashboard.

You make me want to become a cleaner-burning woman.

You make my wheels turn.

You should see my Stop/Start capability.

You're like your hybrid, so quiet but so powerful.

You're so energy efficient.

You're so stealthy in that Prius, I'll show you how to make some noise.

Your back seat or mine?

Your car's power and movement turns my wheels.

Chapter 7: Bumper Stickers For Mechanics

Mechanics like it dirty.

The garage is calling; I must go!

Keep calm: I am a mechanic.

Mechanics love being in different positions on the job.

I may be a mechanic; but I can't fix stupidity.

Keep calm and trust your mechanic.

Mechanics do it with more torque.

If you think it is expensive hiring a good mechanic, try hiring a bad one.

Finally

I hope this book gave you some much deserved laughs.

There's more. I've written several other joke books for other professions too and here are a few jokes from my undertakers joke book:-

Q: Why does the undertaker drive his car slowly?

A: Because he's an undertaker not an overtaker!

Q: If a snake and an undertaker got married, what would their towels say?

A: Hiss and hearse.

Q: Ever heard of the undertaker who accidentally dug up the wrong body?

A: He made a grave mistake.

About the Author

Chester Croker has written many joke books and has twice been named Comedy Writer Of The Year by the International Jokers Guild.

Chester is known to his friends as Chester The Jester and this book is a result of a challenge made to him by one of his friends, a car mechanic, to write a book just for mechanics!

If you see anything wrong, or you have a gag you would like to see included in the next version of this book, please visit the publishers at the glowwormpress.com website.

If you did enjoy the book, kindly leave a review on Amazon so that other mechanics can have a good laugh too.

Thanks in advance.

Printed in Great Britain
by Amazon